Mushroom
Pocket
Field Guide

Mushroom Pocket Field Guide

Howard E. Bigelow

MACMILLAN PUBLISHING CO., INC.
New York

COLLIER MACMILLAN PUBLISHERS
London

Macmillan Publishing Co., Inc.
866 Third Avenue
New York, N. Y. 10022
Collier-Macmillan Canada Ltd.

First Printing 1974

Printed in the United States of America

Library of Congress Cataloging in Publication Data

Bigelow, Howard Elson, 1923-
  Mushroom pocket field guide.
  Bibliography: p. 111
  1. Mushrooms—Identification. I. Title.
QK617.B624   589'.222   73-7682
ISBN 0-02-510650-3

Contents

The Parts of a Mushroom

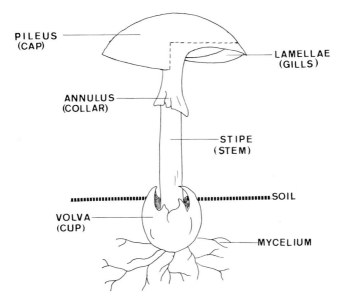

PILEUS (CAP)

LAMELLAE (GILLS)

ANNULUS (COLLAR)

STIPE (STEM)

SOIL

VOLVA (CUP)

MYCELIUM

Life Cycle of an Agaric

1. The spores from the agaric fruiting body are microscopic and usually have one nucleus per spore. Only in large masses, such as in a spore print, can spores be seen by the naked eye.

2. Under favorable environmental conditions, the spores germinate to produce a filament (hypha; plural: hyphae). Nuclear division provides each new cell of the filament with a nucleus like the original one in the spore.

3. The filaments continue to grow if the environmental conditions are favorable.

4. When the filaments of two compatible strains come together, they join to give a binucleate cell which has one nucleus from each of the parent filaments. The binucleate cell divides, resulting in a filament which has binucleate cells.

5. The new type of filament extends itself and branches under favorable conditions, and a mat of filaments (a "mycelium") results in the humus, soil, decayed wood, etc.

6. After the mycelium has grown sufficiently, weather conditions can provoke the production of a fruiting body. Some species produce many agarics at a time; others may have only one. The mycelium is perennial, barring a catastrophe; it continues growth each year and can produce fruiting bodies each year. The fruiting body is mostly composed of filaments like those in the mycelium, except that they are organized in a distinctive manner.

7. On the lamellae (gills) of the agaric are microscopic structures called "basidia." These form the outer layer of each gill. Typically, each basidium produces four spores, and there are thousands of basidia on each gill. The spores are shot a minute distance from the basidium and then fall by gravity. Wind, insects, animals, etc., probably spread the spores further; thus the life cycle can resume in a place far removed from the parent agaric and mycelium.

Other fleshy fungi have a life history similar to an agaric, but the fruiting body and the microscopic details of growth and spore production may differ.

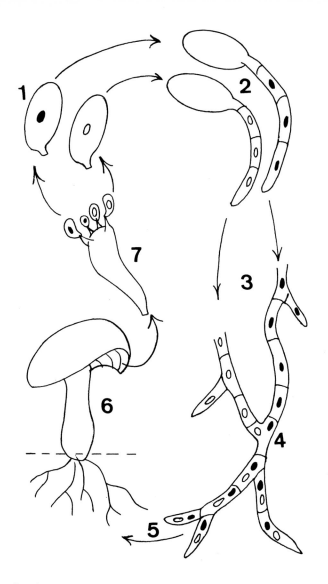

Drawings are not in true proportion to one another. The smallest objects are highly enlarged.

Introduction

Note: THERE ARE NO GENERAL RULES TO TELL AN EDIBLE FUNGUS FROM A POISONOUS ONE. NEVER TRY EATING A FUNGUS YOU CANNOT POSITIVELY IDENTIFY.

In the United States and adjacent Canada, there are several thousand different kinds of fleshy fungi. These include agarics (gill fungi, or "mushrooms" and "toadstools"), boletes (tube fungi), polypores (pore, or bracket, fungi), hydnums (teeth fungi), clavarias (coral fungi), puffballs, earth stars, stinkhorns, and bird's nest fungi. You can discover many of these curious organisms from April into November of most years, and in the warmer regions of North America, they can even be collected during the winter months if there is sufficient moisture. Some people hunt fungi because of a curiosity in the world of nature, others because the fungi have a unique beauty in form and colors, and still another group collects them in order to enhance menus by the unusual tastes of some edible types. The latter pursuit has its hazards, but these are avoidable by using the knowledge and common sense derived from study and observation.

When weather conditions are favorable, some fleshy fungi occur in each of the land habits—lawns, meadows, bogs, sand dunes, alpine tundra, and hardwood and coniferous forests. Certain species may require special substrata such as wood, manure, burned organic material, or the presence of a particular living tree species. Others may be found only during a certain season of the year. Some fruit in large numbers in almost any year, while others seem to be rare, for few are found when these species do fruit. A collector can go back to the same log and find the same fungus year after year on about the same date. On the other hand, another species may be found only once in a spot and never again be seen there. The growth of mycelium and the stimuli for the fruiting of fungi in nature involve combinations of environmental factors which still are not well understood, but any collector can rapidly learn where and when to expect a number of the common fleshy forms. The search always has unpredictable yields in number and variety, and this provides a fascinating study or hobby as well as exercise.

Collecting Fleshy Fungi

The basic equipment for collecting fleshy fungi is simple and inexpensive. A basket is recommended for carrying specimens. Those who have collected thousands of fungi over the years are agreed that a basket is best for this purpose. The size of the basket is strictly a personal choice dictated by the prospects of how much you can, or want to, carry. Some collectors like a basket with a lid—the advantage of this is that it protects the specimens in rainy weather. On the other hand, the lid can be a nuisance and get in the way of a heaping load of fruiting bodies. Bags, whether paper or plastic, are not desirable as a means of transportation because the fruiting bodies are too easily crushed. In addition, the confinement of the specimens in bags will probably soften the tissues, as moisture will collect from respiration and condensation.

A hunting knife or similar garden implement is another item of necessary equipment, for you should always remove the entire specimen from the ground, log, or wherever else it is found. A sufficient number of species have to be dug or cut to warrant carrying a tool for the purpose. The whole fruiting body is necessary for later identification or for the verification of field guesses. The practice of some people of merely collecting the caps for the table is a bad one, for by so doing the base of an *Amanita* could be overlooked. The recognition of the genus and species may depend on this part of the fruiting body and could save you from making a fatal mistake.

It is also important, when collecting, to keep the species separate in order not to confuse the different kinds. This is especially critical if the collecting is also for the purpose of providing food, because a jumble of unwrapped specimens could mix pieces of poisonous ones with edible ones. For this reason, another useful item to take in the field is a roll of waxed paper, which is inexpensive and can be used not only to separate the various species as they are collected, but to protect them as well. Paper, plastic, or sandwich bags have been used by some collectors for these purposes, but such containers are limited in size. Waxed paper, on the other hand, can be adapted to the size of most collections or specimens. A tube of the paper, with the ends twisted, is generally used to wrap small fruiting bodies or collections. Large specimens and collections can be placed between two larger pieces with the four corners of the paper twisted.

When making collections of fungi, label each collection of a species. Indicate on the label the date and place of collection, the tentative name of the specimen (if known), and the name(s) of the collector(s). If desired, notes on color, size, odor, substrate, habit of growth, and other descriptive features can be added.

Making a Spore Print

In order to identify specimens, it is often necessary to obtain a spore print. The color of this print serves as one of the primary characteristics for separating many of the groups of fleshy fungi.

To obtain a print from a mushroom, you must cut off the pileus (cap) at the top of the stipe (stalk), and place the cap, gills down, on white paper. (Colored or black paper is not suitable unless you intend only to make an artistic arrangement of spore prints. The subtle tints of some spore prints are lost on any paper other than white.) The paper with the pileus can then be confined under some type of glass or plastic container of a suitable size. Or a more convenient way is to place the paper and pileus on a sheet of wax paper, and then fold the paper up and over to confine the specimen. Whichever container is used, spore prints are best obtained by excluding air, since air currents move the spores and dry out the pileus.

All pilei will not necessarily shed spores—some may be too young; others, too old. If spores are going to fall from the gills (or teeth, pores, etc.), this can take place rather quickly—perhaps in only two or three hours. Give up on any specimen whose spores haven't collected in a quantity that can be seen by the naked eye after ten to fifteen hours. Experience will teach you how to judge the selection of specimens best suited for prints. Freshness and maturity are critical, but these are not always easy to recognize, even by an expert.

Preservation of Specimens

If you wish to maintain a mycological collection, fresh specimens should be dried promptly and thoroughly after identification or after observations and spore prints have been made; otherwise they will probably become moldy. You will often be disappointed by the loss of recognition characters when many fungi are dried, but there is no other practical means of preservation available to the majority of collectors.

Drying can be done in a container over a layer of silica gel; this method is best for small or fragile fruiting bodies, but probably will not be completely successful for large fleshy types. The larger ones can be dried on screens that are suspended or attached to a frame over heat, using several light bulbs, a hot plate, or a catalytic heater as the heat source. If available, a piece of fireproof canvas çan be wrapped around the frame. The top should be left open, and there should be several inches between the canvas and the floor. In this arrangement the dryer is similar to a chimney, with cool air coming in at the bottom and warm air moving out the top. Warm, circulating air is best for drying the tissue, even though several hours are required. Ovens are not satisfactory, for the specimens are apt to overheat and partially cook.

To avoid crushing the specimens, the most satisfactory way to store them is in boxes. Periodically you should place moth crystals in the boxes, because there are several insects that can get into them and eat the dried specimens. In lieu of boxes, wax paper rolled into cylinders, like those used in collecting, or any type of sandwich bag, can be used. A transparent container is convenient, but you must keep in mind that some plastic boxes are adversely affected when they come in contact with moth crystals and avoid using these.

Poisonous Fungi

To repeat, there are no general rules for determining an edible from a poisonous fungus! The saying that a silver coin will turn black if placed in with a poisonous fungus that is cooking, or remain silver if the species is edible, *is not true,* and anyone who swears by this test has only been extremely lucky. Another old wives' tale with no basis in fact is that if the specimen shows signs of having been eaten by insects or animals, it is therefore safe for humans—you do not know if the insect or animal actually swallowed pieces, or if they did, whether they survived! Still another false tale is that if the top layer of the cap can be peeled off easily it is a harmless type that can be eaten— several very poisonous species of *Amanita* will peel nicely, and if this test has been "proven" by any survivors, it was—again— just dumb luck! Soaking the fruiting bodies in salt water to remove poisons is another erroneous bit of folklore—it will not work when most needed.

Never try eating any fungus you cannot *positively* identify. At present, science does not yet know all the species, let alone their edible or poisonous qualities. You should also be very cautious of consuming even recognizable edible types if there is any sign of discoloration, softness, or insect damage. Mushrooms are subject to rot just like any other vegetable, and people have been poisoned by decay organisms in the mushroom even when there is no toxic substance in the fresh specimen itself.

Mushroom poisoning, suspected mushroom poisoning, or even accidental ingestion of an unknown fungus must never be taken lightly; a physician or hospital should be consulted *promptly* for emergency treatment. The deadly Amanitas may not produce symptoms for six to twenty-hour hours, and the longer treatment

6

is delayed, the less chance there is of survival. Even species which are edible for most people can cause severe allergic reactions in a few sensitive individuals. If you are allergic to some foods (tomatoes, strawberries, shellfish, etc.), the odds are you are allergic to mushrooms. Also, since young children or the elderly may not react to mushroom proteins in the same way as young or middle-aged adults, it is very necessary that they exercise extreme caution in eating edible fungi.

Remember, too, an undue quantity of any food can produce digestive problems, and mushrooms are no exception.

The situation with a particular species may not be simply a matter of whether they are "edible" or "poisonous," for there are many that can be inedible because of a particularly bitter or peppery flavor. Another factor is texture—many species are too tough or too woody to eat. Sometimes these could be successfully softened by excessive cooking, but the result would probably be undesirable—and indigestible. Many tough fungi have never been eaten and may actually be poisonous.

Frequently the experienced collector is asked: "How do you tell a mushroom from a toadstool?" You don't! In my experience people generally call an edible species "a mushroom," and a poisonous one, "a toadstool." On the other hand, I've heard the agarics called "toadstools," while the boletes were "mushrooms"; at other times I've heard the same species called both "a mushroom" and "a toadstool." The terms have no scientific distinction. Both undoubtedly will continue in common usage and common confusion, but it would be preferable to employ terms like "agaric," "bolete," "polypore," etc., if popular generalizations are needed. These refer to taxonomic groups and do not involve the vagaries of edibility.

Agarics

(The Gill Fungi—
Mushrooms and
Toadstools)

AGARICUS CAMPESTRIS (Edible)

This species, often called the "meadow mushroom," is the wild relative of the commercially grown *Agaricus bisporus*. As shown in the plate opposite, *Agaricus campestris* usually grows in grassy places. It may form arcs, or rings, or merely be scattered throughout the grass. Late summer and early fall appear to be the most favorable time for the production of fruiting bodies, although there may be earlier periods of fruiting if the year is generally cool and with abundant rainfall.

When immature (the button stage), the gills are covered by a cottony veil. As the fruiting body expands, the veil breaks and may then form a collar on the stipe. Sometimes, however, the veil clings to the margin of the cap and here forms a fringe, with little of the collar remaining on the stipe. The gills are pinkish at first, gradually turning brown to dark purplish brown as the spores mature. The spore print is purplish brown.

When collecting for the table, the beginner must avoid the button stages unless there is clear assurance by very close mature specimens that the species is actually *Agaricus campestris*. In the button stage the deadly *Amanita*, as well as *Lepiota naucina* or other species of *Agaricus*, may be confused with *Agaricus campestris*. This could lead to tragedy.

AMANITA BISPORIGERA (Deadly poisonous)

Three pure white Amanitas, all very poisonous, are not uncommon in the woods and nearby vicinities. To the naked eye, *Amanita virosa* and *Amanita verna* look about the same as *Amanita bisporigera,* and they can only be distinguished by microscopic characters identified by an expert. All have a white spore deposit, an annulus, and cuplike volva, but the latter may not be obvious without careful observation. Most of the volva, along with the stipe base, is immersed in the soil and humus, and even the top free edges may be obscured by fallen leaves. This characteristic alone is reason enough never to collect mushrooms just by cutting off the caps in the field, for the important structures indicating that these are deadly species will thereby be overlooked.

The deadly *Amanita phalloides* of Europe, which has a dull olive-green pileus, has been found growing in the San Francisco area and also in Pennsylvania, Delaware, New Jersey, New York, and Virginia. Probably this species is more widespread than is known at present.

Poisoning by *Amanita bisporigera* or closely related Amanitas is extremely serious, and medical help must be obtained promptly. Survival depends on the rapidity of professional treatment, even though illness may not be apparent. By the time symptoms of poisoning occur (six to twenty-four hours), it may be too late to save the victim. The poisons in the fruiting bodies *are not* destroyed by cooking, drying, freezing, or any other known means of preparation.

The names "destroying angel" or "death angel" are often used as common names for the deadly white Amanitas, particularly *Amanita virosa.*

AMANITA BRUNNESCENS (Poisonous)

The wedge-shaped base of the stipe of *Amanita brunnescens* is one of its distinctive characters; this same-shaped base is also found in the whitish *Amanita aestivalis* (called by some *Amanita brunnescens* form *pallida*). Both are common in the Northeast, and both are believed to be poisonous. When the stipe of either is bruised, there is a slow change in color to dark red or reddish brown. This color change might lead the beginner to think that he has collected the nonpoisonous *Amanita rubescens*, but the latter has a club-shaped stipe base and usually many warts on the cap (see plate on page 21). The three really do not look much alike, but the color changes that they have in common serve to emphasize the warning that the beginner must not rely on a single character in trying to identify agarics.

The pileus of *Amanita brunnescens* is olivaceous brown and often appears rather radiate-streaked from fibrils. At times there may be a few white patches of volva on the cap surface, with other patches remaining on the soil surrounding the stipe base. The annulus is white, membranous, and superior, but occasionally adheres in irregular patches to the margin of the cap instead of forming an annulus. The spore deposit is white.

AMANITA CAESAREA

There are few gill fungi more beautiful than this *Amanita,* but it doesn't seem to be common except in small local areas. Oak woods apparently are the favorite habitat, although on one occasion I found fruiting bodies in an open mixed woods of hemlock, beech, birch, and maple, with no evident oaks about. Most of my collections have been made during August or early September.

Amanita caesarea (Caesar's mushroom) is actually an edible species, but the beginning collector should not attempt to eat it because of the possibility of confusing it with one of the poisonous Amanitas. The plate opposite shows the button covered by the white universal veil, partial expansion of the pileus and rupture of the veil, and an expanded specimen with the universal veil at the base of the stipe as a cup (volva). The pileus may be scarlet, reddish orange, orange, or sometimes nearly yellow. As with other Amanitas, the spore deposit is white.

AMANITA FLAVORUBESCENS (Dangerous—edible or poisonous qualities unknown)

Amanita flavorubescens can be confused with *Amanita muscaria* as well as *Amanita rubescens* if the collector is not careful to note the character of the volva. In *Amanita flavorubescens* the volva is yellow and breaks up into pieces. Sometimes the fragments are on top of the pileus, but more often they remain on the soil at the base of the stipe when the fruiting body expands. The bright yellow cap of fresh specimens fades out rapidly in sunny or dry weather or in age. I have not found that this species reddens as much as *Amanita rubescens,* but some staining is usually present on the stipe base, both inside and out. Both species have a white spore print.

Amanita flavorubescens appears to be most common in the grassy edges of open hardwood stands, but on a few occasions I have found it on lawns or in a meadow quite some distance from any trees. Other woodland Amanitas with yellow volval fragments are *Amanita flavoconia* and *Amanita frostiana* (not illustrated). The pileus of both species is bright orange or sometimes yellow, but neither species stains reddish on the base of the stipe. As in the case of *Amanita flavorubescens,* the edible or poisonous qualities have not been determined positively for these two species.

AMANITA MUSCARIA (Poisonous)

In most years *Amanita muscaria*, or the "fly mushroom," is common in a variety of habitats. The brightly colored caps, with flecks of white or pale yellow particles, have made this species familiar to many observers of nature. Usually the caps are yellow to orange in the Northeast, bright red in the West, the South, and Europe. Sometimes very expanded specimens of the yellow form may have a reddish orange center. If washed by heavy rains, the caps may lose their warts and appear smooth. Usually there is a distinct annulus hanging from the upper portion of the stipe, but sometimes the specimen expands atypically so that this collar is ruptured peculiarly and hangs from the edges of the cap. The universal veil does not form a distinct cuplike volva as in some Amanitas, but contributes instead to the warts on the top of the cap and forms rather cottony or membranous rings and patches near the base of the stipe. These remains can be difficult to find on weathered specimens. The spore deposit is white.

    Amanita muscaria is associated with several types of trees, and though frequent in woods, only one tree is necessary for fruiting bodies to occur. On several occasions I have seen a lawn with only one large pine and a circle or arc of many specimens of *Amanita muscaria*. The householder can therefore find this poisonous agaric growing in his front yard, thus creating a potentially dangerous situation for curious small children.

AMANITA RUBESCENS

The surface and flesh of this *Amanita* redden upon bruising or in age, and therefore the appearance of expanded specimens is often quite different from that of buttons. The plate opposite illustrates the color form that is probably most likely to be encountered in the Northeast. The warts on the surface are characteristic, but they are easily washed off in the rain. No cuplike volva is present at the base of the stipe as in some Amanitas.

This species is edible, but should not be sampled by beginners as it may be confused with poisonous species. *Amanita rubescens* grows in hardwoods, sometimes most singly or sometimes as groups of several fruiting bodies. The pileus may reach a diameter of six inches at times, and the total height of the plant may be eight to ten inches high.

Also see plate and accompanying text below.

HYPOMYCES HYALINUS

The plate opposite shows an *Amanita rubescens* which has been parasitized by another fungus, *Hypomyces hyalinus.* The agaric has been distorted in shape and color, and never has the usual gills and spore production. At first this infected form is whitish; but as the parasite matures, the overall surface color changes to a pale dingy wine color. The interior flesh bruises the characteristic reddish color of *Amanita rubescens.*

A curious aspect of this relation between the two species is that normal and infected forms of *Amanita rubescens* can be found a few feet or even a few inches from one another. Sometimes apparent intermediate stages of infection are found, but usually the agaric seems to become affected from the button stage. There are reports that the infected form is as edible as the normal *Amanita rubescens,* but eating such specimens is extremely risky, as some of the poisonous species of *Amanita* are also known to support the growth of *Hypomyces hyalinus* upon occasion. For example, I have found *Amanita bisporigera, Amanita muscaria,* and *Amanita flavorubescens* infected with this parasite.

ARMILLARIA MELLEA (Edible)

This species, commonly called the "honey mushroom," has a cap color that varies from yellow to brown. Usually there are minute scales on the cap and a collar on the stalk, at least in young specimens. Dozens of caps can grow together in large clumps about stumps or even living trees. Sometimes you may find hundreds in a small area under either hardwoods or conifers. If a tree or stump is not visible, certainly buried wood is present and the fruiting bodies are connected to the wood by microscopic filaments. Though edible, this agaric can be destructive to living trees by causing rot. The rot can spread to uninfected trees by black stringlike strands which the fungus is capable of producing.

The spores of *Armillaria mellea* are white or cream in a spore print. *Omphalotus illudens,* which also grows with wood, has similar spore prints; but it has bright yellow to orange colors and no ring on the stalk. You should be very sure of correctly distinguishing *Armillaria mellea* from *Omphalotus illudens* if your interest is in a wild mushroom for the table, because the latter species is poisonous.

CANTHARELLUS CIBARIUS (Edible)

The Chantrelle can occur from early summer into fall in the woods. The features for recognition are an overall yellowish to orange color, with the gills and stipe usually somewhat paler than the pileus. The flesh is thick and pliant; the gills are decurrent (extending downward), very narrow with a blunt edge, and often with interconnecting small veins; the spore deposit is yellowish. The pileus ranges from about one to three inches across, and the whole plant is from one to four inches high.

Good moist seasons will produce many specimens of this fungus, and many times I have seen them in numbers ranging from dozens to over a hundred.

The collector of table mushrooms must learn to distinguish *Cantharellus cibarius* from *Cantharellus floccosus* and *Hygrophoropsis aurantiacus* (not illustrated). The latter two species have not been proven safe for all people. *Hygrophoropsis aurantiacus* has bright orange gills which are close and thin.

CANTHARELLUS FLOCCOSUS

The bright colors and large size (up to eight inches tall and five inches across) of the vase-shaped fruiting bodies of this fungus often present a startling sight in the woods. Inside the funnel are large scales. In age the orange color fades out to a dingy buff, and the scales are often washed down into the base of the funnel. The gills are not distinct as in true mushrooms, but are instead foldlike or veinlike down the length of the fruiting body.

Opinions seem to vary on the edible qualities of *Cantharellus floccosus*. Fatal poisonings are not known, but some people have experienced severe upset stomachs after eating them. Others report the fungus as being very tasty and safe. Perhaps individual allergies are involved, so if you wish to eat this species, try only a small quantity at first to determine what the effects might be. Better still, stick with a species that you know agrees with you.

Another large species which could prove confusing is *Cantharellus kauffmanii* (not illustrated). It is similar in stature to *Cantharellus floccosus,* but has a tan-colored cap with brown scales. Nothing has been reported thus far about the edibility of *Cantharellus kauffmanii.*

CLITOCYBE CLAVIPES (Edible)

Clitocybe clavipes typically is found during the fall collecting season, most commonly under white pine. The fresh pileus is a watery brown or gray brown, the gills whitish to pale cream, and the stem is a dingy white. The base of the stem is usually club-shaped and often connected, or rather interwoven, with the surrounding pine needles. It is considered an edible species, although opinions vary as to its desirability as a choice eating mushroom. The texture is likely to be soft, and the frequent presence of small tunnels in the flesh testify to early occupancy by fly larvae.

Clitocybe is represented in most woods by several common species during the summer and fall, but adequate information about their edibility is lacking. Some have been tested and found to contain toxic compounds, even though these are present in small amounts. *Clitocybe sudorifica,* a whitish species, occurs on lawns and other grassy places in August and September, and is definitely known to be poisonous. Families with small children at the age when eating is apt to be indiscriminate should be certain to remove all fungi from around the home area.

CLITOCYBE GIBBA (Edible)

This summer agaric is quite common under hardwoods or in stands of mixed pine, hemlock, beech, birch, and maple. A related species, *Clitocybe squamulosa,* has similar stature, brown cap and stipe, and is more frequent in the pure conifer stands of northern regions. In some mushroom books, both species have often been included under the name *Clitocybe infundibuliformis.* Little is known for certain about the edible qualities of *Clitocybe squamulosa,* but at least no definite poisonings have been assigned to it.

The characteristic vase-shaped cap of *Clitocybe gibba* is pinkish tan, but the intensity of color varies according to age and exposure. Older caps subjected to bright sunlight and rains fade to yellowish or even white. The flesh, gills, and stipe are whitish, and a spore print will be white. In size the cap usually measures up to two and a half inches across, and the total height may reach five inches. If you should come across fruiting bodies under hardwoods that look like *Clitocybe gibba* but are considerably larger and more robust, you have probably found *Clitocybe maxima*. This is rare in the New England area, but is not infrequent in the Great Lakes region or in the Pacific northwest. *Clitocybe maxima* has been reported as edible in Europe, but it is not known whether North American specimens are safe to eat.

CLITOPILUS ABORTIVUS (Edible)

Clitopilus abortivus is a very unusual species because it grows in two distinctly different forms—one a typical and normal-appearing "mushroom," and the other an abortive type which resembles small cauliflowers. In the fall both forms can occur under hardwoods or conifers, but the abortive one seems to be more abundant. Both are edible, but if you are collecting for the table, you must be cautious when collecting the normal one. Unless specimens are attached to, or very close to, the abortive form, they should not be eaten. There are several poisonous species that look very much like the normal form and have similarly colored spore prints. However, these poisonous species do not produce the irregular fruiting bodies of *Clitopilus abortivus*.

The normal *Clitopilus abortivus* has a gray cap, and the gills become a dull grayish rose color as the spores mature. The spore print is pink to pale rose in color. The cap may be as much as four or five inches broad; the stipe may run to three inches long and a half inch thick. The other form is whitish overall on the outside, whereas the inside is often mottled or streaked with a pale buff or pinkish color. Individual fruiting bodies are one to three inches across, but may grow in clumps which may be a foot or more across.

COLLYBIA DRYOPHILA (Edible)

This is a common agaric throughout most of North America, and fruitings may contain large numbers of caps. Sometimes *Collybia dryophila* grows singly or as a few scattered caps, but more often there are clumps or groups. The habitat is not too specific, although one usually finds this agaric in the woods on leaf mold under broad-leaved trees. Rotten logs and wood chips may also yield fruitings. Mixed woods of conifers and hardwoods or conifer plantations are possible habitats too. Under the conifers in the fall, the collector is more apt to encounter *Collybia butyracea,* another edible species.

The colors of the cap and stipe of this white-spored agaric are variable, and consequently can confuse the inexperienced collector. Some forms have dark brown caps and stipes, while others have a light yellowish brown to buff-colored cap and a reddish brown stipe; still another form has a brown cap and a whitish to yellowish stipe. However, the narrow, crowded gills of all the common forms of *Collybia dryophila* are whitish, and the flesh is thin, pliant, and whitish. The caps usually range from one to two and a half inches across.

Collybia dryophila may fruit almost any time during the growing season of agarics.

COPRINUS COMATUS (Edible)

The "shaggymane," infrequent during hot and dry weather, may be found in open grassy places from May into October. Particularly good fruitings may contain one to two hundred fruiting bodies, much to the joy of those who like to eat this species. Generally, however, you will find only a dozen or so at a time, and it is not unusual to find successive crops in the same spot if favorable moisture and temperatures prevail.

The recognition characters are the cylindrical white pileus, with brownish scales; gills that melt into a black ink; and a white stipe with a movable annulus. As in all of the inky caps (*Coprinus*), the gills of *Coprinus comatus* are whitish at first. When spores begin to mature, the gills and cap edge begin to darken from the bottom of the cap upward. The self-digestive enzymes turn the tissue into a black liquid that drips off and carries the spores to a new spot for germination and growth.

Many collectors prize this species as one of the tastiest of the edible fungi. The younger caps with white gills are the best for eating. Old caps, partially "melted," have caused digestive upsets in some people.

COPRINUS MICACEUS Group (Edible)

Several species in North America masquerade under the name
Coprinus micaceus. They are very similar in general appearance,
with the differences mainly in microscopic characteristics. As far
as is known, all are edible when young and fresh. Mild stomach
upsets can result if "melting" caps are eaten, though.

The inky caps are fairly common in clumps on or near
hardwood stumps, and they are often one of the first mushrooms
to appear in the spring. Repeated fruitings may occur on the
same stump during the growing season, but especially in the
early fall. Buried wood, as well as stumps and logs, also supports
their growth. You don't have to go into the woods to hunt this
group, as curb lawns with elm and maple stumps frequently
have many fruiting bodies.

CORTINARIUS ARMILLATUS (Edible)

In August and September *Cortinarius armillatus* is frequently
found under conifers. However, if weather conditions are
especially favorable, fruiting may take place during July or as
late as October.

This is an edible species, well tested by mycophagists, and it
is unlikely to be confused with any other *Cortinarius*. Besides the
reddish brown or reddish tan pileus, pale cinnamon to rusty
brown gills, brown spores, and cobwebby veil, *Cortinarius
armillatus* has several red zones, or rings, on the stem. These red
rings usually persist through all stages of the fruiting body,
although of course the texture of the larger caps and probable
insect residents make them unsuitable for the table. The
measurements of this species usually are: cap one to five inches
broad, stem two to six inches long. The typical stem base is
club-shaped; the gills, broad.

CORTINARIUS OBLIQUUS

The genus *Cortinarius* is the largest genus of the gilled fungi, and hundreds of species can be found in the United States and Canada. Some occur in practically every habitat at one time or another, but they are most frequent on the ground in woods. The variety of colors, shapes, and textures exhibited by the various Cortinarii make for fascinating hunting and viewing, but the majority of species are very difficult for a beginner to identify—even experts have problems with them. Some species can be found that do not have names as yet, and for many there is no accurate available information on the edible or poisonous qualities. It is not known whether or not *Cortinarius obliquus* is poisonous.

Cortinarius obliquus illustrates one of the fairly common delicately tinted species. Characteristic of the genus, *Cortinarius obliquus* has brown spores and a cobwebby veil. Expanded fruiting bodies do not usually show the delicate fibrils of this veil, and one must have the button stage to be certain the veil is present. In the field some species of the related genera—for example, *Inocybe* and *Hebeloma*—can be difficult to distinguish from *Cortinarius*.

GALERINA AUTUMNALIS (Poisonous)

An old wives' tale holds that all mushrooms growing on wood are edible. Though this may be true of the majority of wood-inhabiting species, the brown-spored *Galerina autumnalis* and *Omphalotus illudens* are two common agarics that refute this tale: they grow on logs and stumps but *are* poisonous. Large numbers of *Galerina autumnalis* are frequently found in the fall, and if you are tempted to eat them, remember that such a meal has proved fatal to a few people. No rule-of-thumb can be employed to distinguish edible from poisonous kinds!

Galerina autumnalis has a moist brown cap which may be slimy when fresh. The gills are yellowish at first but become brown. A veil covers the young gills, and this veil breaks to form a collar on the stem.

HYGROPHORUS CONICUS

The genus *Hygrophorus* contains a number of species which are conspicuous by their bright colors. Other species, which are white or dull-colored, are often difficult to identify. All species in the genus have white spore deposits and gills with a waxlike luster.

While some species of *Hygrophorus* are known to be edible (though their small size generally makes them impractical for cooking), *Hygrophorus conicus* (see plate opposite) must be regarded as too risky to eat because it has not yet been clearly established whether poisoning cases can be attributed to it. Nor have a number of other Hygrophori common in the woods during summer and early fall been tested for edibility. Therefore you should not experiment with any of these in the naive belief that some edible species in a genus make the whole genus safe. *Hygrophorus conicus* is one contrary example, and there may be others.

The fruiting bodies of this species blacken in age or with bruising, and this is a convenient means for identifying them in the field. Usually the cap is distinctly conic, but the color may vary from yellow to orange or to bright red before blackening. When young, the gills are white; in age they become orange to yellow, often with an olive tint. The stipe is fragile and, like the cap, can vary in color; but most commonly it is olive yellow.

LACCARIA LACCATA (Edible)

If there is a species comparable to a "weed" among the mushrooms, it is *Laccaria laccata*. Fruiting bodies can occur in any month of the growing season, and in just about all habitats. This species grows in the woods, on lawns, in bogs, and even on the tundra areas of Mount Washington, New Hampshire, and Mount Katahdin, Maine.

The beginning collector can be easily confused by the variable features of this agaric. The color of the cap and stipe may be flesh color to orange cinnamon, but it soon fades to whitish or pale buff. Sometimes young fruiting bodies may have violet tints. The gills are flesh color at first but often darken to deep reddish tones. The gills are also broad, widely separated from one another, and notched at the stipe or slightly decurrent. The pilei usually range from a half inch to two inches broad, and the total height of the fungus may be from three-quarters inch to four inches. The spore print is white. Sometimes single specimens occur, but more frequently they are found in groups of several or many. They are slow to decay.

LACTARIUS VELLEREUS (Dangerous—edible or poisonous qualities uncertain)

The genus *Lactarius* is recognized in the field by the latex which is exuded when fresh specimens are cut or broken. Depending on the species, the juice may be white, yellow, orange, or even blue. In some the color may change on exposure to the air, or the latex may stain the flesh various shades. At least three hundred kinds occur in the various habitats throughout the country, and many are edible when properly cooked. Some Lactarii have strong, biting tastes which are too much for the mouth to tolerate, but this unpleasantness can often be removed by parboiling. These sharp-tasting ones should never be eaten raw.

Three species of white Lactarii are found abundantly— *Lactarius deceptivus*, *Lactarius vellereus* (shown in plate opposite), and *Lactarius piperatus;* all have a biting taste, white milk, and dry caps. *Lactarius deceptivus* has a thick cottony margin on the cap; *Lactarius vellereus* has yellowish gills which are widely separated; and *Lactarius piperatus* has crowded, flesh-colored gills. These three are by no means the only white ones, but they are the most common.

LACTARIUS HYGROPHOROIDES (Edible)

This *Lactarius* occurs from July into September of most years, although I have seldom found large numbers at any one time. In size, the species is moderate, with a cap up to three or four inches across. The gills are widely spaced, and when broken, exude an abundant white milk. A spore deposit will be white.

Another species has similar colors—*Lactarius volemus*. This one, however, has close gills, and they bruise brownish. It is also edible, so no harm results if it is confused with *Lactarius hygrophoroides*. Both species seem to prefer open woods of broad-leaved trees.

LEPIOTA NAUCINA

Many mushroom guides list this white *Lepiota* as edible, but two warnings are quite necessary. Some people cannot eat it without experiencing a severe digestive upset that lasts several hours. While the attack is not known ever to have been fatal, it is not worth the pleasure of tasting a wild mushroom dish. Of a more serious nature is the possibility of confusing *Lepiota naucina* with the deadly *Amanita verna, Amanita virosa,* or *Amanita bisporigera.* All are white, with a collar on the stem. The latter three have a distinct cup (volva) at the base of the stem, but this cup is embedded in the soil and could be overlooked. *Lepiota naucina* grows on lawns and in other grassy places in the fall, while the Amanitas are usually found in woods during the summer. However, one tree on a lawn can be responsible for the fruiting of Amanitas, and a warm wet September easily can prolong their occurrence.

LEPIOTA PROCERA (Edible)

Lepiota procera is usually large (eight to fifteen inches tall) and easy to spot along the grassy edges of roads. I have also found fruiting bodies in open woods and in pastures. August and September seem to be the typical months for growth; rarely does one find more than a half dozen caps in a small area.

The recognition features for *Lepiota procera* are the brown or reddish brown scales on the expanded pileus; a small blunt umbo (a rounded bump on the center of the pileus); free white gills, broad near the edge of the cap margin; long brittle stipe, with scaly or scurfy coating; bulbous base; movable superior annulus; white spore print. Not all people find all Lepiotas edible, and one must be certain of species identification. For example, *Lepiota molybdites* has been responsible for poisonings. This species is common in grassy areas in the southern United States, but it has been found in southern New England and across to lower Michigan. The spore print and older gills of *Lepiota molybdites* are a dull greenish color. These features, of course, cannot be observed in buttons, so identification of *Lepiota molybdites* can be tricky before growth reaches the expanded stages. I do not know of fatal poisonings from Lepiotas, but have heard of episodes of misery which were not worth the experiment.

MARASMIUS OREADES (Edible)

This agaric, common on lawns and other grassy areas, is commonly called the "fairy-ring mushroom," although a number of other species can form circles of fruiting bodies in the same fashion. *Marasmius* has the quality of reviving when rewetted, and thus the same caps can contract and expand over a period of many days before finally decaying. The stipes are quite tough and can be a nuisance to the care of a lawn even after the caps have been removed by a mower.

You should not rely upon the ring formation to recognize *Marasmius,* for it can be scattered, not only in small groups but in arcs as well. The color of the cap is usually cinnamon to buff or light brown, but orangy or reddish tones may be present. In time the caps fade to cream or pale buff with a flesh tone. The stipes are similar in color and have fine hairs over the surface. The gills are whitish, broad, fairly distant from one another, rounded next to the stipe, and nearly free. A spore deposit will be white.

OMPHALOTUS ILLUDENS (Poisonous)

This specimen can be recognized by the bright yellowish orange to orangy-yellow colors, narrow decurrent gills, and its growth in clumps on or near hardwood stumps. In age, the color of the caps and stipe often become paler or duller, but that of the gills remains bright for some time.

If the gills of *Omphalotus illudens* have the proper physiological condition, the curious phenomenon of phosphorescence can be observed in them. Young and rapidly expanding specimens seem best for observing a glow which, of course, must be seen in a dark place. When phosphorescence is present in the gills, it is very obvious; indeed, the glow is of such intensity that on one occasion I was able to read a newspaper near a large clump and to see the outlines of the gills through the tops of the caps. Further, the glow will continue even if the phosphorescent specimens are removed from their place of growth.

August and September seem to be the most favorable months for finding this species. Fruitings are widely scattered, but where they are present there are usually large numbers of caps. Sometimes you may find specimens that seem to be growing on soil; in these cases the mycelium is probably attached to the roots of a previous tree near the site.

Other mushroom books may treat this agaric under the name *Clitocybe illudens*. The common name "jack-o'-lantern" obviously is derived from its phosphorescent qualities.

PANAEOLUS CAMPANULATUS

In order to find this black-spored agaric, you must hunt in pastures, barnyards, near stables, or in other heavily manured areas. Horse or cow dung is necessary for the growth of this species; it will not be found on humus in the woods, although the dung of wild animals will probably permit growth.

The fruiting bodies are fairly tall—sometimes up to six inches. The pileus may be as large as two inches in diameter, but more often it is about an inch wide. The color is an olivaceous gray that fades out to dingy tan in age and with loss of moisture. The gills are broad, subdistant, adnate (connected on one side) to the stipe but easily broken away. They are grayish at first with a white fringed edge, and the sides become blackish and rather spotted as the spores mature. There is a grayish coating over the stipe at first, but the color beneath is brown. The stipe breaks easily, and the caps are fragile.

The edibility of this agaric is uncertain, and of course the substrate of manure creates a considerable problem as far as cleanliness is concerned. This species is not recommended!

PANAEOLUS FOENISECII

Appropriately, the "haymaker's mushroom" grows in grassy places—throughout the warmer seasons of the year if there is plenty of moisture. Sometimes in late May and early June there may be hundreds of fruiting bodies on large lawns or in park areas. Pastures and meadows may also harbor this species, but it may well be overlooked in the taller grass. This *Panaeolus* is edible, but it cannot be recommended because of the possibility of its being confused with some other less well-known species that have caused mild poisonings in some people.

In color, the caps are a brown to vinaceous brown, sometimes with a purplish cast. They fade fairly rapidly in the sun, and usually end up looking a dingy pale buff. The gills are a pale chocolate color for some time, gradually darkening to a dark vinaceous brown as the spores mature. Stipes are grayish brown to brownish. Other characteristics that will aid recognition of *Panaeolus foenisecii* are: adnate or rounded gills, broad, close to subdistant; tubular and brittle stipe; and very dark brown spore print (not black as in *Panaeolus campanulatus*). The species is generally small with caps up to about an inch broad, and stipes one and a half to three inches long.

PHOLIOTA SQUARROSOIDES (Edible)

The spore deposit of this wood-dwelling agaric is rusty brown in color, and the fruiting bodies are found on hardwood stumps, logs, or stubs. Beech and maple seem to be especially favorable substrates. In most years August and September are the months to hunt for this species, although one may occasionally find it in July or October. Usually large clumps of fruiting bodies occur, with caps ranging in size from one to three inches broad.

The features of the fruiting bodies that are relevant for recognition are the numerous tawny-brown scales on a whitish to pale-buff cap and stalk, a slimy layer beneath the dry scales, habitat on wood, and brown spores. The gills are whitish at first but gradually darken as the spores mature. The gills are attached to the stalk and are also broad.

The buttons of *Pholiota squarrosoides* are supposed to be the best of all mushrooms for the table. There are a few other scaly Pholiotas that grow in the Northeast, and all are edible as far as is known. However, most mycophagists do recommend removing the slimy layer from the caps before cooking—not because the layer is believed to be poisonous, but because the texture is unpleasant.

PLUTEUS CERVINUS (Edible)

To find specimens of *Pluteus,* the collector must hunt on various woody substrata. Sawdust piles, logs, and stumps of both conifers and hardwoods can support fruiting bodies. Usually these occur first in the spring and then again in the fall, in conjunction with the wetter periods of the year. Single caps can occur, though sometimes you may be fortunate enough to discover many in one place.

The caps are blackish at first, then become grayish brown to buff with a violaceous tint. The gills change from white to pinkish, and finally to a dingy rose color as the spores mature. The stipe is whitish, but may have black-brown fibrils at the base. Rarely does the cap exceed three to four inches. The overall height of the plant may reach five inches.

RUSSULA Species

The genus *Russula* includes many brightly colored species that are common and conspicuous during the summer months. Mild-tasting species are regarded as edible, but the peppery ones are controversial. Some people claim the latter are edible if properly cooked, but others tell of having had unpleasant experiences after eating them. A taste test of *Russula* can be made by chewing a small piece of cap on the tongue in the forepart of the mouth. It will be almost immediately obvious if you've got a peppery species, and if you have, don't swallow the chewed fragments.

This genus is easily recognized in the field, but species are difficult to distinguish except by an expert. *Russula emitica* (not illustrated) is one of several bright-red ones that could easily be confused with an edible species. *Russula emetica* has a sharp biting taste, viscid cap with striate margin, white gills and stipe, and a white spore deposit. The red of the cap may fade to pink or white in age, especially if exposed to considerable sun or rain. All authorities warn against eating *Russula emetica*.

Shown in the plate opposite is *Russula veternosa*.

Boletes

(Tube Fungi)

BOLETINELLUS MERULIOIDES (Edible)

Acquaintances of mine who have eaten this bolete judge the flavor and texture to be second-rate and decidedly inferior to many other species. This is unfortunate, for many caps can be found wherever ash trees grow. I have observed dozens about a single tree on lawns as well as in the woods. Old ones persist for many days and get quite moldy or soft from bacterial decay—and, of course, the species should never be eaten when it is in such a deteriorated state.

The pores of *Boletinellus merulioides* are larger and the tubes are shallower than those of most boletes. When bruised, the yellow pore surface becomes olive, then reddish brown. There should be no possibility of confusing this with any other species.

BOLETUS EDULIS (Edible)

This bolete occurs in the summer and fall, usually in August and September, and it is one of the tastiest of edible fungi according to all reports. This species is the *steinpilz* of German cookery, and the cèpe of French cookery. The button stages are best, although one often has difficulty finding any stage that is free from worms. Fruitings take place under coniferous trees.

The cap color ranges from tan to rather dark yellow-brown or reddish brown. The tubes are whitish when young, but gradually change to greenish yellow. The stalk is whitish to pale tan, often bulbous and with a fine network over the upper portion. No portion of the fruiting body becomes blue to green when cut or bruised.

BOLETUS FROSTII

The deep-red colors and coarse network on the stipe make this one of the most beautiful of boletes. In addition, there are startling changes in color when the flesh and tubes are cut or bruised. Mature fruiting bodies show the quickest change to blue. They are usually found in oak woods during July and August.

Opinions vary about the edibility of boletes that have red tube mouths and/or that turn blue on bruising; some people have become ill on these. On the other hand, some mycophagists claim any bolete can be eaten and have tried all except those with a bitter taste. Apparently, then, individuals vary in their reactions to eating this group, and for that reason it has to be considered dangerous. I personally know of no fatal poisonings, but several acquaintances have reported severe stomach upsets.

LECCINUM ATROSTIPITATUM (Edible)

The field characters are: a dry, pale, dull orange-brown cap; whitish tubes; and a white stipe with brown to blackish points. The flesh of the cap is thick and firm, white but staining grayish to blackish when cut. The stipe interior may also change to bluish green at the base. This is one of the larger boletes; the cap may reach eight inches across, and the stipe can be five inches long and perhaps two inches thick.

Leccinum atrostipitatum occurs under hardwoods, but there are related species of the same general coloration which may also be found in hardwoods or under conifers. All are edible when fresh. Accurate identification of these species may not be possible, but there are no hazards when collecting for the table.

SUILLUS AMERICANUS (Edible)

This bolete is fairly abundant under white pine in the late summer and fall. When fresh, the pileus and stipe are bright yellow. The tubes are also yellow, but become duller in age and stain brown when bruised. Young pilei have a fringe or patches of cottony veil-material along the margin. In addition, the pileus is viscid, often with streaks of reddish fibrils. No annulus is present on the slender stipe, but there are small irregular brown dots.

The flesh is rather thin and soft, and frequently riddled by larval tunnels. However, since the species often grows in large numbers, one can usually find a sufficient number of small caps which do not have guests.

In size, the pilei are one to four inches broad, the pores are broad (to about one-tenth inch), the stipes are up to four inches long and one-half to three-quarters inch thick.

SUILLUS GREVILLEI (Edible)

Suillus grevillei is found near or under larch trees in late summer and fall; it does not occur under other conifers. Single fruiting bodies may be found, but more frequently there are several or many which form arcs, or rings, on the needles beneath the tree. The cap is slimy, and if it is to be eaten, the slimy coating should be peeled off before cooking. The color of the cap can be yellow or orange to reddish brown. The tubes are dull yellow, then tinted with olive; they do not turn blue on bruising but instead become reddish brown. An annulus is present on the upper part of the stipe, except perhaps in overmature fruiting bodies. The absence of glandular dots on the yellow stipe helps to separate this species from several other common boletes.

Large caps of *Suillus grevillei* may reach six inches in diameter, but usually they are about three to four inches when expanded. Buttons will have the tubes covered by the down-curved cap margin and attached annulus. The stalk is about one and a half to four inches long, and up to one inch thick.

Hydnums

(Teeth Fungi)

HERICIUM CORALLOIDES (Edible)

When fresh, this species is white and looks very much like a cluster of small icicles hanging from a log or a tree wound. The size of the fruiting body is variable. It may be as small as two inches across, and three inches long; but usually it is from four to eight inches broad and long. Luxuriant fruitings may result in several clumps of even larger size on one log. Hardwood logs, especially large ones of beech, are the usual substrates, and you should be on the lookout for the fruitings from July through September particularly.

Some mycophagists prize this member of the tooth fungi as a great delicacy. Old fruiting bodies that have yellowed or become brown in places should not be eaten. Decay, or at least poor flavor and texture, are indicated by discoloration.

HYDNELLUM DIABOLUS

The size of the caps and the quantities in which they sometimes occur may tempt one to speculate on the possibilities of eating this type of tooth fungus. However, most are far too tough to chew, much less digest. Many also have strong odors and tastes.

Species of this genus and related ones are most common under conifers during the late summer and fall. Among the more glamorous species are: *Hydnellum aurantiacum,* with orange stipe and cap; *Hydnellum geogenium,* with sulfur-yellow stipe, teeth, and cap margin; *Hydnellum suaveolens,* with blue stipe, bluish zones on the flesh, and an intriguing heavy, sweet odor.

When the caps of *Hydnellum diabolus* are fresh and the weather is moist, the caps are dotted with drops of pink-red liquid. Young specimens have a pinkish felt over the whole cap. Later this coating is confined to the margin, and the center becomes brown. The odor is pungent and farinaceous, while the taste is bitter and farinaceous.

DENTINUM REPANDUM (Edible)

The general shape of *Dentinum repandum* is similar to an agaric, but instead of gills on the underside of the cap, there are numerous teeth. The color of the cap is a light orange to brownish, and the stipe is white or tinged with the cap color. A related species is white overall, while another has teeth the same color as the cap. Some forms have a stem which bruises yellowish or orangy. All these have a mild taste and are edible, but many of the stalked tooth fungi have either a bitter or strong unpleasant taste and are too tough to eat.

Dentinum repandum is common in both coniferous and hardwood forests, but you will rarely find many fruiting bodies close together in a small area. I have collected the species from July through October in some wet years.

Clavarias

(Coral Fungi)

CLAVARIA Species

The coral fungi are not uncommon during the summer and fall in moist woods of all kinds. Most grow on the forest floor, but *Clavaria pyxidata* (not illustrated) occurs on logs and stumps.

The branched species may form large clumps that can measure a foot or so across. Others are fingerlike, club-shaped, or almost threadlike, and these may be quite small and fragile. These species often form many individuals, even though the mass of the single fruiting body is slight. Both branched and single forms include white types or those which are colored yellow to orange, purple, reddish, or rose color.

Tests to date indicate that, in general, the clavarias seem to be edible. There is little information about the edible qualities of the fragile, slender species, though, because attempting to cook them would be quite impractical. The more massive species have a history of having caused diarrhea in some people. It is not known for sure whether the people so affected were allergic to the fungus, whether the specimens were too old, or if there was actually a poison in the species. *Clavaria gelatinosa* (not illustrated), which grows in the western United States, is reported to be poisonous.

Polypores

(Bracket, or Pore, Fungi)

POLYPORUS VERSICOLOR

This wood-rotting pore fungus may be found at any time of the year, although the fruiting bodies may not be fresh and from the current year's growth. Because of its tough nature, *Polyporus versicolor* endures longer than agarics, but usually produces spores only for one season. Insects will gradually devour the fruiting bodies. They may also be covered by mold or algae in age. Fresh ones are notable by the multicolored bands of gray or brown on top—because of these bands some people call them "turkey tails." The underside is white to creamy and perforated by many small pores or tubes where the spores are formed. The texture of *Polyporus versicolor* makes it unsuitable for the table.

Large numbers of this polypore can occur on logs and stumps. Sometimes the fruiting bodies are layered like shingles; or, if the position is right, they may form rosettes. Their presence on fence posts or on structural timbers means that the wood is rotting and will soon have to be replaced.

POLYPORUS SQUAMOSUS

Some mushroom books list this species as edible, but usually this polypore is much too tough to chew or digest. Very young fruiting bodies are edible, according to some of my friends, but it would seem that rigorous cooking would be necessary to soften up older ones. As with some other tough or woody polypores, the question of human consumption is not one of poisons but rather of palatability or practicality.

Polyporus squamosus is quite common on the stumps of elm and maple in urban areas, but fruitings also take place in the woods. Usually the first ones appear in May or June, but they can occur later in the summer or fall. One particular elm stump I know of has been producing three crops of fruiting bodies a year for about five years.

The maximum size of the cap is rather indefinite, but one often sees caps of twelve to eighteen inches across. Old and large specimens soon deteriorate from the action of insects and molds.

FOMES APPLANATUS (Not edible)

The "artist's fungus" is perennial, or at least it can form a
new tube layer each year for several years. Rarely do they
last beyond six or seven years, however, as insects usually
invade and destroy the fruiting body. In size, the conks
(fruiting bodies) are often a foot in diameter, but they may
reach three feet across. Large trees frequently have several
—if high on a trunk and inaccessible to the passerby. Most
commonly, *Fomes applanatus* will be found on logs and stumps,
but it does grow from wounds in living trees. A number of
broad-leaved trees and conifers can be affected. The
appearance of a fruiting body on a valuable shade tree should
be viewed with concern, for this means that decay of the wood
is present.

   Fomes applanatus is too tough to be edible but, as the
popular name suggests, it does have a use for those who are
artistically inclined: during the summer and early fall, there is
a white powdery coating over the young tubes that can be
removed by a needle or other sharp pointed instrument to
make a sketch or design.

FOMES

Jelly Fungi
and Relatives

TREMELLA Species

Members of the jelly fungi, such as species of the genera *Tremella* or *Dacrymyces,* are frequently encountered on decaying wood. They are not a food source because of their small size and unpleasant texture, yet the bright yellow and orange colors often provoke the curiosity of even the casual observer of nature. In dry weather the fruiting structures will dry and shrink, but when rain comes again they can reabsorb water and expand. Some naturalists refer to these forms as "witches'-butter."

TREMELLODENDRON SCHWEINITZII

The beginner often confuses this fungus with a coral fungus (a *Clavaria*), but the texture is tough instead of soft or crisp; and though most coral fungi are edible, the *Tremellodendron* could cause a digestive problem if eaten by mistake. No poisonings are known to have occurred from it, but its toughness would make it an undesirable item for the menu.

The growth of *Tremellodendron* is quite slow, and several weeks are required before it reaches the branched condition and coloration shown in the plate opposite. You will usually find this fungus on soil in the woods.

The reason why *Tremellodendron* is placed with the jelly fungi is not apparent from its appearance in the field. The microscopic details of spore production have provided the clues to the relationship.

AURICULARIA AURICULA (Edible)

The texture of this curious fungus is quite rubbery, but—perhaps surprisingly—it is an edible species. *Auricularia* doesn't seem to be as common as some books suggest; however, when it does fruit, numerous caps are often produced. Occasionally, I have found hundreds nearly covering a log. Growth is always on decaying wood, and fruiting takes place in summer and continues into fall. The logs and stumps of either coniferous or broad-leaved trees are suitable for the growth of *Auricularia.*

    The tan-colored specimen in the plate opposite is placed to show the spore-producing surface. This hangs downward from the log or stump. The upper sterile surface of the fruiting body is brown and is covered with very fine hairs. With some obvious justification, folklore fancies the fruiting body as resembling the ear of a human. Its true relationship is with the jelly fungi.

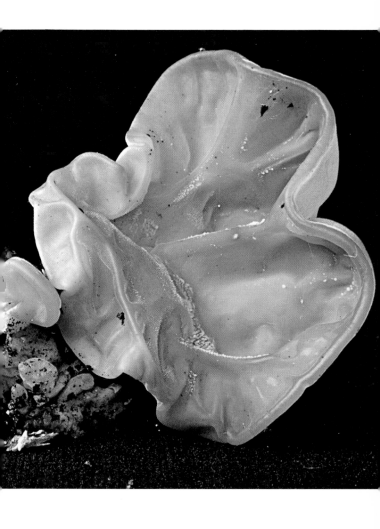

Puffballs

CALVATIA CYATHIFORMIS (Edible)

Lawns and meadows are the typical environments for this species as well as for a number of other puffballs. Most occur in August and September shortly after the first fall rains. Three large puffballs with a smooth surface are not infrequent: *Calvatia cyathiformis* (shown in the plate opposite), *Calvatia craniformis,* and *Calvatia gigantea.* When the spores are mature and the inside dusty, *Calvatia cyathiformis* is purplish within, while the latter two are yellow brown to olive brown. *Calvatia craniformis* and *Calvatia cyathiformis* may be six inches broad, but the less common *Calvatia gigantea* will be larger (eight to fifteen inches).

All these large puffballs are edible when they are white inside, but they should *not* be eaten when they begin to turn yellow inside and form spores. If left in place for a few days after discovery, puffballs may enlarge further, but you risk their becoming mature, decaying in part, or harboring insects.

LYCOPERDON PYRIFORME (Edible)

Lycoperdon pyriforme is found near or on decaying logs and stumps, or occasionally on sawdust piles. Sometimes you may find a mere handful; but, not uncommonly, there may be hundreds. When white and firm within, the pear-shaped puffball is edible and considered tasty. When young, it is a good safe species for a beginner; but as soon as the inside of the fruiting body begins to yellow, it should not be eaten, since the yellowing indicates that spores are beginning to develop. Eventually, when the spores are mature, the entire interior is a dusty mass of brownish olive. Usually the outside of the puffball is brownish, but it can be whitish to yellowish as well. There are very fine scales or granules over the surface. In size, the single fruiting bodies range from a half inch to one and a half inch.

SCLERODERMA AURANTIUM (Not edible)

Although closely related to edible puffballs, *Scleroderma aurantium* has caused unpleasant experiences for some mycophagists who ate it. Thus it must be excluded from the list of fungi recommended for eating. There should be no difficulty in distinguishing this *Scleroderma* from the Calvatias and Lycoperdons, however, for the wall is much thicker and tougher in the former. In addition, *Scleroderma,* which is hard and firm inside, soon turns black, and is not pliant and white as are the young *Calvatia* and *Lycoperdon*.

   Scleroderma aurantium grows on soil, humus, or rotten wood, and can be found in the woods and in bogs. For several years I have had fruitings on my lawn near a birch tree. *Scleroderma* also seems to be common in the picnic areas of state parks, sometimes parasitized by *Boletus parasiticus.*

Bird's Nest Fungi

CRUCIBULUM LEVIS

From the plate opposite, you can see how the common name, "bird's nest fungus," was derived. The spores are formed within the "eggs" (peridioles), and these develop within a cup. After the membrane that covers the cup has ruptured, the peridioles will be moved from the cup by rain splash.

Crucibulum levis and another common species, *Cyathus striatus* (not illustrated), may be found in a variety of places in the summer and fall. Usually the fruiting structures are attached to fallen twigs and branches or leaves. Sometimes rather odd substrata are involved; for example, I have found *Crucibulum* on old discarded leather and paper goods. The bird's nest fungi are not eaten because of their small size (up to about a half inch) and tough texture.

Stinkhorn

DICTYOPHORA DUPLICATA (Not edible)

The common name of this fungus is "stinkhorn," and once you have found it you will agree it is well named. The odor is so strong in fresh specimens that you can locate them in the woods by their smell alone. However, if the green slimy mass at the end has been removed by flies, the odor is virtually absent.

Immature specimens of stinkhorns are shaped like eggs, and are whitish and often tinged reddish or brownish. In this stage, a collector could mistake them for edible puffballs; but, when sliced, the stinkhorn egg will show an inner layer of jelly. The mature fruiting body expands rapidly, rupturing the egg. In temperate regions *Dictyophora* is distinguished from other stinkhorns by its hanging veil.

This species is found during the late summer into October, usually in wooded areas.

Earth Star

GEASTRUM TRIPLEX

Although the texture of these fungi discourages much interest in their use as a food, their unusual form is always intriguing. Appropriately, the common name is "earth star." The plate opposite shows an unexpanded fruiting body on the left. As development proceeds, the outer layer splits and curves back to form the points of the star. The spores are contained in the center sack and are ejected through the pore upon pressure.

Earth stars can be found in the woods on soil and humus. Some related types occur in open sandy places. In size, *Geastrum triplex* may be as large as four inches from point to point, but is more likely to be two to three inches across.

Morels and
Cup Fungi

MORCHELLA ESCULENTA (Edible)

Morels, a favorite of mushroom fanciers, are found in the spring of the year. Sometimes they occur as early as April and as late as middle June, but usually they are most prevalent during May. A number of habitats can produce fruiting bodies, although folklore holds that an apple orchard is the favorite spot. Morels do occur in orchards, but also in conifer plantations, open hardwood stands, in fields or their borders, and even in gardens. Specimens occur singly, in small groups, or occasionally in large numbers when the spring is particularly wet. However, an element of luck seems to be involved in finding morels, for their appearance in a seemingly favorable place is not a certainty.

As the plate opposite shows, *Morchella,* with its numerous irregular pits, resembles a sponge. There is no other fungus that morels really resemble, although sometimes beginners confuse them with *Gyromitra esculenta,* which can also occur in the spring. However, *Gyromitra esculenta* has a darker and more reddish brown cap, and the pileus is not pitted like morel but resembles a brain or consists of lobes (see below).

GYROMITRA ESCULENTA

In the springtime—late April through May and sometimes early June—this species, called the "false morel," may be found in coniferous woods. The color is reddish brown, and the cap has ridges and wrinkles rather than the pits of the true morel. Other species of *Gyromitra,* or *Helvella,* are not easy to distinguish from *Gyromitra esculenta,* and several can occur in New England during the spring. The beginner should avoid all but the obvious true morel, as the edibility and poisonous record on Gyromitras and Helvellas is a confused one. Some people have been poisoned in the past, but it is not clear in all cases whether this was due to individual reaction, decayed fruiting bodies, or poisons in the fungus. For species identification of the Gyromitras or Helvellas, consult one or more of the books listed in the Bibliography.

HUMARIA HEMISPHAERICA

The plate opposite shows enlarged cups; normally they are less than an inch in diameter. The spores are produced in the inner white part of the cup, and as with other cup fungi, may be ejected violently in a fine whitish cloud.

The edibility of the species is unknown; but even if not harmful, it is not a desirable eating species because of its small size and scanty growth. Undoubtedly *Humaria's* breakdown of organic debris serves a purpose in nature's cycles; but for man, the fruiting bodies are mainly an object of beauty and curiosity. The occurrence of the cups is not predictable, and in some years even the most careful searching will fail to turn up any. I have come upon them only occasionally, and then on very decayed logs in the woods.

URNULA CRATERIUM (Not edible)

This odd cup fungus fruits during the spring months of April to June and is not uncommon in woods of broad-leaved trees. However, because of its rather dingy and camouflaging colors, it may well be overlooked by a collector. Usually it can be found growing next to a log. Solitary specimens are frequent, and only occasionally does one find several specimens in one place.

In size, *Urnula craterium* may be as small as one inch in diameter or as large as three inches. Not evident in the plate opposite is a short stipe that has black hairs at the base. Immature cups are somewhat paler on the outside, and the hymenium inside is dark brown rather than black. Old or weathered specimens are black overall.

MITRULA PALUDOSA

Mitrula paludosa grows in cool wet places during the spring and early summer. It is not unusual to find fruiting bodies partially submerged in the shallow water of mountain streams and in seepage areas which are fed by melting snow. The stipes are usually attached to sticks and leaves.

The plant reaches a height of about two inches. The yellow cap and short white stipe have a soft texture; but despite this, the fruiting bodies are quite persistent. Gradually the bright yellow will fade out to a pale dingy buff.

There doesn't seem to be any information about the edible or poisonous qualities of this ascomycete. Probably its small size and rather delicate flesh have not provoked the interest of mycophagists, or else any that were cooked couldn't be found after preparation!

SARCOSCYPHA COCCINEA (Edible)

These scarlet cups are about the first fleshy fungi to appear in the spring, although finding them can be a challenge. Often they are hidden under fallen leaves, and you need a little luck to catch a glimpse of their red color against the brown of winter debris. In size, the scarlet cup may be as small as a half inch or as large as two inches.

When fresh and mature, these and other cup fungi will discharge spores violently. A puff of whitish spores can be triggered by blowing on the inside of the cup or even, at times, by stamping on the ground near the cups. If they are brought home and put on damp toweling in a covered container, a cloud of spores may result when the cover is abruptly removed.

Selected Bibliography

Groves, J. Walton. *Edible and Poisonous Mushrooms of Canada.* Ottawa: Research Branch, Canada Department of Agriculture, Publication no. 1112, 1962.

Hesler, L. R. *Mushrooms of the Great Smokies.* Knoxville: University of Tennessee Press, 1960.

Krieger, L. C. C. *The Mushroom Handbook.* Reprint. New York: Dover Press, 1968.

McKenny, Margaret and Stuntz, Daniel E. *The Savory Wild Mushroom.* Rev. ed. Seattle: University of Washington Press, 1971.

Miller, O. K., Jr., *Mushrooms of North America.* New York: E. P. Dutton, 1972.

Pomerleau, R. *Mushrooms of Eastern Canada and the United States.* Montreal: Les Editions Chantecler, 1951.

Smith, A. H. *The Mushroom Hunters Field Guide.* 2d ed. Ann Arbor: University of Michigan Press, 1963.

————. *Mushrooms in Their Natural Habitats.* Reprint. Portland, Oreg.: Sawyers, 1949.

Thomas, W. S. *Field Book of Common Mushrooms.* New York: G. P. Putnam's Sons, 1948.

NOTE: A number of books in German, French, and English are also available from Europe and Great Britain. Excellent as many of them are, the species included may not be found in North America.

Picture Glossary

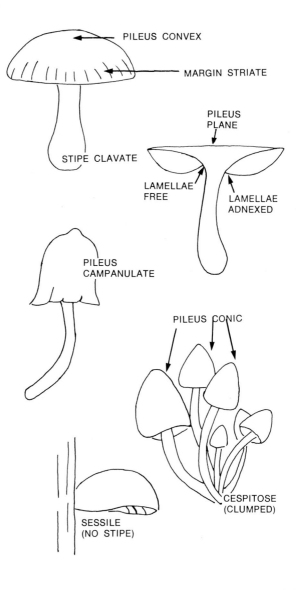

PILEUS CONVEX

MARGIN STRIATE

STIPE CLAVATE

PILEUS PLANE

LAMELLAE FREE

LAMELLAE ADNEXED

PILEUS CAMPANULATE

PILEUS CONIC

CESPITOSE (CLUMPED)

SESSILE (NO STIPE)

Picture Glossary

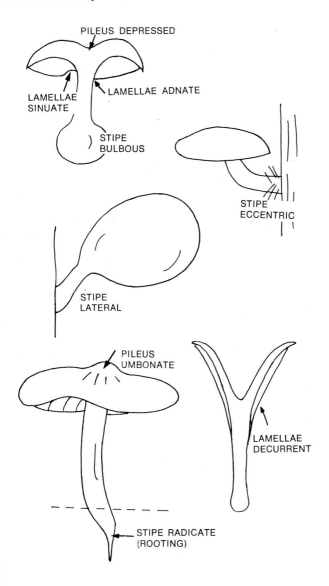

Index

(Page numbers in boldface indicate those on which photographs appear.)

116